Young Artists of the World™
Argentina

Marianela Forconesi's Painting: "My Father's Farm"

Jacquiline Touba, Ph.D. and Barbara Glasser
in collaboration with the IACA World Awareness Children's Museum

The Rosen Publishing Group's

New York

The young artist's drawing was submitted to the International Youth Art Exchange program of the IACA World Awareness Children's Museum. You are invited to contribute your artwork to the museum. For more details, write to the IACA World Awareness Children's Museum, 227 Glen Street, Glens Falls, NY 12801

Acknowledgments: Maria Cristina Espandin; Gretchen Stein.

Published in 1997 by The Rosen Publishing Group, Inc.
29 East 21st Street, New York, NY 10010

First Edition

Book Design: Erin McKenna

Photo Credits: p. 4, 7 © W. Bertsch/H. Armstrong Roberts, Inc.; p. 8, 9 © B. Bachman/Camerique/H. Armstrong Roberts, Inc.; p. 11 © Kummels/Zefa/H. Armstrong Roberts, Inc.; p. 12 © K. Scholz/H. Armstrong Roberts, Inc.; p. 15 © H. Abernathy/H. Armstrong Roberts, Inc.; p. 19 © St. Meyers/Zefa/H. Armstrong Roberts, Inc.; p. 20 © Camerique/H. Armstrong Roberts, Inc.

Touba, Jacquiline.
    Argentina: Marianela Forconesi's painting "My Father's Farm" / by Jacquiline Touba and Barbara Glasser.
        p.   cm. — (Young artists of the world)
    Includes index.
    Summary: The young Argentine artist, Marianela Forconesi, discusses the culture and landscape of Argentina and describes a painting she made while spending time on a farm.
    ISBN 0-8239-5100-6
    1. Forconesi, Marianela—Juvenile literature. 2. Child artists—Argentina—Biography—Juvenile literature. 3. Farm life in art—Juvenile literature.
    [1. Forconesi, Marianela. 2. Children's art. 3. Argentina—Social life and customs. 4. Farm life.] I. Forconesi, Marianela. II. Glasser, Barbara.
    III. Title. IV. Series.
    N352.2.A7T68 1997
    982.06'4—dc21
                                                                                                          96-54495
                                                                                                             CIP
                                                                                                             AC

Manufactured in the United States of America

Contents

My Country

My name is Marianela Forconesi. I am from Argentina. My country is in the southern part of South America. The southern tip of Argentina is only 500 miles away from cold Antarctica. But the northern part of my country is hot and **humid** (HYOO-mid). The center of Argentina is a **plain** (PLAYN) called the **pampas** (PAHM-pahs). The pampas has a mild **climate** (KLY-mit). Many plants grow in this area because of the climate.

The high Andes Mountains lie on the border between Argentina and another country called Chile. These mountains are more than 5,000 miles long and stretch through four other countries.

Marianela Forconesi

◀ The Andes Mountains make up a huge mountain range that runs between my country and Chile.

The People

Some of the first foreign people to come to Argentina were Spanish **explorers** (ex-PLOR-erz). Later, people from other countries also came to live in Argentina. While many different kinds of people live in my country, we are all Argentines and speak Spanish.

Gauchos (GOW-chohz) also live in Argentina. Like cowboys in the United States, gauchos herd cattle in my country. Gauchos wear **ponchos** (PON-chohz). A poncho is a square piece of wool cloth with a hole cut out for a person's head. During the day it is worn as a coat. At night the poncho is used for a blanket.

Ponchos are made out of warm, colorful material. ▶

My City

I live in a city called **Villa Constitucion** (BEE-ya KOHN-stih-too-SYOWN). It is located along the Paraná River. My city is about 125 miles away from **Buenos Aires** (BWAY-nohs AY-reez). Buenos Aires is the capital of Argentina. It is on the Rio de La Plata. Big ships travel up the Paraná River to Villa Constitucion from the Atlantic Ocean.

In Villa Constitucion, the most popular sport is football, which is called soccer in the United States. We also have art schools and a special center for dance, theater, and music in my city.

Sometimes airplanes from the big city of Buenos Aires fly over our farm.

◀ Buenos Aires is much larger than my city of Villa Constitucion. Twelve million people live in Buenos Aires.

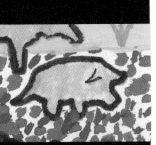

We raise pigs on our farm in the country.

The Country and the City

While many people live in the cities, there are also large farms and cattle ranches in my country. Most of these farms and ranches are in the pampas. **Shepherding** (SHEP-erd-ing) is found in the mountains. Beef and wool are important products in Argentina, along with crops like wheat and corn. Oil is an important **resource** (REE-sorss).

In the cities there are large businesses where people work. Many families who live and work in these cities also have small farms. There they can raise their own crops and animals, like my family does.

Many of the people who live in Buenos Aires also have homes and farms in the country. ▶

My Family

I live with my family in two places. During the week, we live in the city of Villa Constitucion. On the weekends, we live on our farm. It is located about fifteen miles away from my city.

I have a sister named Vanesa Laura. She is one year younger than me. My mother is a homemaker. My father works with his brother on the farm.

I would like to study **agricultural engineering** (AG-rih-KUL-cher-ul EN-jin-EER-ing) when I get older. I also like to play tennis. Someday I would like to travel to other countries.

◄ My brother and father work on a farm, just like these men do.

My father takes care of our crops when he works on the farm.

13

The Farm

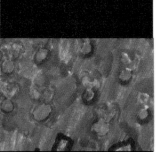

One of my jobs at the farm is to put **lime** (LYM) on the trunks of the fruit trees. You can see the ripe apple tree in the middle of my father's farm. I also feed the animals and collect eggs. We have sheep, cows, pigs, chickens, turkeys, and rabbits on our farm. My grandfather made the **trough** (TROFF) that the pigs use.

We grow crops such as **calabash** (CAH-lah-bash), squash, watermelons, corn, soybeans, **sorghum** (SOR-gum), wheat, oats, lentils, and sometimes green peas.

Like these apples, the apples from our tree on the farm are bright red. ▶

People in My Picture

I was eight years old when I drew this picture of my father's farm.

In my picture, I am lying in the sun on an orange blanket. My father is raking leaves under the apple tree. He puts his rake and other tools in the round grey tool sheds at the back of the picture. My mother is watering flowers with a watering can. She loves to work in her garden. My sister Vanesa Laura is playing with a balloon. One of my cousins has picked some flowers for his mother. Another cousin is scraping mud off his shoes by banging them against a tree.

Everyone in my family has chores to do. But there is plenty of time for all of us to do fun things too.

◀ In my painting, you can see all the different things that happen on my family's farm.

When I'm in the country, I like to lie in the sun on my favorite orange blanket.

Birds in My Picture

I feel very close to nature when I spend time on the farm. I wake up with the sun and the chirping birds. Small, brown birds called sparrows often fly around the farm.

In the apple tree, you can see the nest of the ovenbird, which is a bird from Argentina. The ovenbird's nest is made of clay.

My favorite bird is the owl. The one in my painting is asleep. Owls sleep during the day and are awake at night.

Owls are nocturnal. That means they eat and fly during the night and sleep during the day. ▶

The Seasons

It is summer in my picture. I drew some of the beautiful flowers that grow on our farm, such as **freesia** (FREE-zjah) and daisies. It is summer in Argentina from December 21 until March 21. Argentina is in the southern **hemisphere** (HEM-iss-feer). It is summer here when it is winter in countries in the northern hemisphere, like the United States. All of our seasons are the opposite of the seasons in the northern hemisphere.

◄ We have daisies like these on our farm.

There are flowers all over the garden. My mother takes good care of them.

¡Hasta Luego!

Someday, I hope you can visit my country. You can spend the weekend with my family and me on our farm. We can do all sorts of fun things there. I can show you the apple tree with its delicious apples. We can also feed the animals together. And you can meet all of the members of my family. We might even see the owl when it gets dark.

¡Hasta luego! (AH-stah loo-AY-go). That means "see you later" in Spanish. I hope I will see you sometime soon.

Glossary

agricultural engineering (AG-rih-KUL-cher-ul EN-jin-EER-ing) A way of using science to grow and sell crops.

Buenos Aires (BWAY-nohs AY-reez) The capital city of Argentina.

calabash (CAH-lah-bash) A large, hard-shelled gourd used for holding things.

climate (KLY-mit) The weather in a certain part of the world.

explorer (ex-PLOR-er) A person who discovers new places.

freesia (FREE-zjah) A sweet-smelling flower.

gaucho (GOW-choh) A Spanish cowboy.

¡Hasta luego! (AH-stah loo-AY-go) "See you later" in Spanish.

hemisphere (HEM-iss-feer) One half of Earth.

humid (HYOO-mid) Damp or moist.

lime (LYM) A white substance made when limestone is burned.

pampas (PAHM-pas) A flat area where many plants are able to grow.

plain (PLAYN) A long, flat area of land.

poncho (PON-choh) A type of cape worn or used by a gaucho.

resource (REE-sorss) Something in nature that is bought and sold.

shepherding (SHEP-erd-ing) Taking care of sheep.

sorghum (SOR-gum) Grain that is used in making cereal.

trough (TROFF) A long container that animals eat and drink from.

Villa Constitucion (BEE-ya KOHN-stih-too-SYOWN) A city in Argentina.

Index